Time for Preschool

Time for Preschool

An Early Developmental Tool
Designed for Toddlers
Ages 1-2

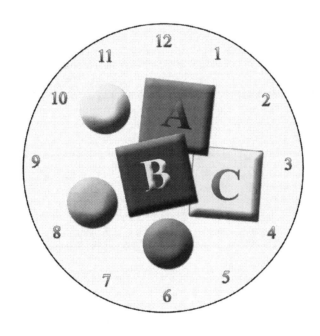

Written and designed by:

Susan Sellmeyer

iUniverse, Inc.
Bloomington

Time for Preschool
An Early Developmental Tool Designed for Toddlers

iUniverse books may be ordered through booksellers or by contacting:

iUniverse
1663 Liberty Drive
Bloomington, IN 47403
www.iuniverse.com
1-800-Authors (1-800-288-4677)

ISBN: 978-1-4620-4470-2 (sc)
ISBN: 978-1-4620-4471-9 (ebk)

Printed in the United States of America

iUniverse rev. date: 02/07/2013

CONTENTS

Finally, a preschool program for one—and two-year-olds!

- Want to give your child a boost on his or her education?
- Discouraged because day-care centers don't offer a program for your child?
- Don't have much time? That's okay!
    o Great for on-the-go or working parents
    o Only forty-five minutes a day!
- Flexible program that can be customized to: o Meet the needs of your child's development o Meet the needs of the parents schedule
- Simple and easy-to-use at-home curriculum

The curriculum presented in this book is designed for toddlers ages one to two years. Children ages two to three may also benefit from this curriculum, depending on their knowledge of the material presented. *A Time for Preschool* is split into sections representing each day of the week and provides a focus for a particular subject on each day. The book begins with a note to the parents, a list of quick tips, and then an overview of the curriculum. Each section provides an objective page, a how-to section, and a checklist that is relevant to that particular subject. Additional material is included at the end of the book, providing age-appropriate games, arts and crafts, and optional materials to purchase or make.

Susan Sellmeyer was born in 1976 and grew up on a small farm in eastern Kansas. Susan attended a junior college near Kansas City, earning two degrees in information technology. Later becoming a mother of a premature child, Susan strived to learn everything she could about brain development. When her daughter was one year old, Susan began designing a curriculum to teach her daughter basic preschool material at a very young age. Susan customized the material to fit the needs of her young child and a busy working mother's schedule, while still pursuing a full-time career in information technology. Today Susan is still teaching her daughter and striving to give her daughter every educational opportunity she can.

About This Program

This preschool curriculum is designed for toddlers ages one to two years. Children ages two to three may also benefit from this curriculum, depending on their knowledge of the material presented.

This curriculum focuses on seven subjects that are to be introduced on different days of the week. Not only is this curriculum designed for very young children, but it is also designed to offer the flexibility to fit your child's needs and abilities, as well as your need for time in a busy world. You are encouraged to spend forty-five minutes a day with your child on the planned subject for that day, using focused play and interaction. That's it! You need only forty-five minutes a day, and there are no expensive setup costs or materials to buy. However, at the end of this book, there is a list of basic preschool materials you may or may not choose to purchase. You are encouraged to use homemade materials as much as possible and utilize things already in your home that can be converted into learning tools.

This curriculum was first introduced to a one-year-old child who was born two months premature. The curriculum was designed by the child's mother, who was a full-time working mom who didn't have a lot of free time but wanted to give her child an early boost in educational development. After following this curriculum for one year, this child could do all of the following:

- identify over fifty different animals and tell you what most of those animals ate
- correctly identify all the letters in the alphabet (both uppercase and lowercase) and recite the alphabet in order from A to Z
- correctly identify the numbers one through twenty, count out loud to ten, and count up to ten objects
- identify all the basic colors in addition to more advanced colors, such as gold, silver, and violet, and tell you which colors mixed together would make green, orange, and purple
- identify all the basic shapes, including identifying the difference between an octagon and a pentagon

By using intentional focus and manipulation of activities and spending forty-five minutes a day with your child, you'll be not only giving your child an educational boost but also bonding with your child as you both learn and grow. It will be your job as the teacher to *intentionally* focus on one subject for that time and then follow through with that focus by manipulating what books are read/viewed, what videos are watched, and what activities are done. Learning is an ongoing process, and much of what a toddler learns is through repetition. That is why this program focuses on the same seven subjects each week and encourages parents to follow through with that subject in the day-to-day activities of their toddler's life.

The other huge advantage of this program is flexibility. Because the focus is on the same seven subjects each week, you will have the opportunity to customize this program to fit the needs of your child based on what your child already knows. For instance, every week this program delegates time toward the subject of animals. If your child already knows all the barnyard animals, move on to zoo animals or sea creatures. The point is, there is time dedicated each week to learning about a particular subject; however, the content of that subject may change based on the development of your child. The other advantage is that the program requires only forty-five minutes a day and can also be taught on the go. For instance, if you have errands to run, that's okay. Don't feel you have to be strapped down to the house because of a preschool lesson. Take it with you! For numbers day, you could count to your child in the car or count how many stoplights you go through. If you need to go to the grocery store, count the number of items you are purchasing or point out the different colors and shapes of the fruits and vegetables. Perhaps it is a gorgeous day outside, so take it outside! Draw numbers or animals on the sidewalk; talk about the animals you hear and see. The point here is *focus*. Focus on that subject for that day, and then follow through with it, whether it's at home or on the go.

*** One last note: *make it fun!* Children learn through play. When something is forced upon a child, he or she will not respond positively to it and frustration will set in for both you and your child. Don't worry about getting frustrated, because it will happen. The thing you have to realize is that this is your focus, not your child's. It is very hard for a child at this age to stay focused on anything for any amount of time, so you are the one who has to stay focused. Follow your child's lead and move from room to room (area to area) instead of trying to confine your child to a table or one area. The key to this program is interacting with your child through focused play, not forceful actions. If it is numbers day and all your child wants to do is play with his or her barnyard set, then go with it. Start counting the animals! Count their feet or compare how many legs the animals have to how many legs we have! The same goes for when it's animal day and all your child wants to do is play with the food from his or her play kitchen. Talk to your child about what animals eat carrots or lettuce, etc. Again, the key to this program is interacting with your child through focused play. *So have fun, improvise, be creative, and don't be afraid to be silly. Children love it when grown-ups act goofy!* ***

*** Remember, if your child (or you) is not feeling well, it is no time for trying to learn; it is a time for comforting and compassion. The well-being of you and your child, along with safety, should always come first.

Disclaimer

There is no guarantee that comes with this curriculum, as children learn at different rates and it is up to you, the parent (teacher), to work with your child. This curriculum is simply a guide and a tool for you to use to engage in your child's early learning development.

Quick Tips

Before you begin this program, please read these quick tips.

- ❖ Know what your child knows.
    - o Periodically test your child's knowledge and skills.

- ❖ Keep a log of what your child has accomplished and what your child still needs to work on.
    - o A weekly bulletin board works great for this.
    - o Use the checklists provided to help you keep track.

- ❖ Never force this curriculum or any other curriculum on your child.
    - o If your child is not willing to cooperate, take a break and introduce the material at a different time.

- ❖ Children learn at different rates. If your child is experiencing difficulty with a particular item, move on to something else and come back to that item at a later time.

- ❖ Let your child know that it is time for preschool: announce, "It's time for preschool," or ask, "Do you know what time it is?"
    - o Follow a routine so your child knows that after certain events happen, it is time for preschool.
    - o Creating a routine will help children get in the mind-set for preschool and give them a sense of control, as they know what to expect next.

- ❖ Keep distractions to a minimum during preschool time. Try to limit the following:
    - o Guests in the house
    - o Noisy family members
    - o Phone calls
    - o TV

- ❖ Plan ahead. Figure out what you will be working on and get all the materials and supplies ready before preschool begins.

- ❖ Show your child different instances of the same object. Allow your child to experience the object in different sizes, shapes, and colors.
    - o When possible, show your child different types of the same object.
        - ▪ Example: different types of dogs, cats, cows, flowers, etc.

- o Present both real-life pictures and cartoon images of the same object.
- o Allow your child to use as many senses as possible.
  - ▪ For instance, when presenting a flower, you can
    - see it,
    - touch it, and
    - smell it.

❖ Have fun! Enjoy your child and the time you are spending together. Get up, dance around, or act silly. Do whatever it takes to present the material in a fun, upbeat fashion so both you and your child get the most out of the learning experience. More than likely, if you are not having fun, your child will not have fun and will not be interested in what you are doing or what you are trying to teach him or her.

Curriculum Overview

- Motor Skills Mondays

- Colors and Shapes Trivia Tuesdays

- Animals Gone Wild Wednesdays

- Thinking Numbers Thursdays

- Fun Fridays

- ABCs Saturdays

- Sunday School Sundays

Music Time Anytime!

Motor Skill Objectives

Importance:
Motor skills are the ability to move one's body in a series of learned movements to produce a smooth, refined action. There are two main types of motor skills:

- Gross motor skills: large muscle movement (e.g., sitting up, crawling, walking, running, jumping, stomping, kicking/rolling/throwing a ball, etc.)

- Fine motor skills: small muscle movement, usually to perform a precise task (e.g., grasping objects with thumb/index finger, transferring objects from one hand to another, picking up small objects, placing objects out of a container, threading beads, etc.)

Goals:
To help your child master new skills to advance his or her interactions with people and objects, which enhances social and physical development

Material Explanation:
Checklist of motor skills to work on with your child, including a blank area for you to add motor skills you would like to work on with your child
List of action words to focus on and check off as your child *understands* each word and its action

The How-Tos of Motor Skills

Be creative! Look at your child's toys and figure out which toys your child cannot yet play with by him—or herself. On Mondays, break those toys out to play with and help your child master them. Perhaps it's a puzzle, a music box, rings on a cone, or stackable cups. Go around the house and find buttons to push, things to move, objects to pick up, etc., to teach your child how the real world works (for instance, turning a light switch on/off). Please remember to keep safety in mind at all times and don't teach your child how to hurt him—or herself (for instance, don't teach your toddler how to jump off the bed)!

On Mondays, put the entire focus on motor skills, whether it's all day or just the forty-five minutes you set aside specifically for preschool. Let your toddler do things that aren't in the everyday routine:

- Let your toddler practice drinking from a cup without a lid, at mealtime or outside.
- Allow your toddler to play on the computer with you.
- Manipulate your toddler's toys by breaking out the toys he or she still needs to master or needs more practice with.
- Play games, such as Follow the Leader, Simon Says, or a matching game.
- Ask your toddler to touch various body parts: eyes, ears, legs, feet, etc.
- At story time or bedtime read a book about movement, such as people or animals playing, dancing, etc.
- If TV or videos are allowed, allow your child to watch a short show involving movement.
- Take your child to a park or indoor play area as a field trip.

The idea here is for you, the teacher, to focus on activities and play to enhance what your child can learn to do with his or her body. I encourage you to spend forty-five minutes of quality time with your child and focus on activities related to motor skills and helping your child master new skills. Use the suggested motor skill checklist to practice these movements, and the action word list to teach your child these actions and their reactions. Add your own motor skills and action words in the spaces provided. Follow this up by watching a video and/or reading a book related to movement.

*** Remember, every child is different and everyone learns at different rates. If your child is not mastering a particular skill or becoming frustrated with trying, move on to a different skill and come back to that one later. The motor skill checklists are in no particular order, so you can tailor them to your child as time will allow and as your child's skills develop.

Motor Skills Mondays

Motor Skill Checklist
- ❑ Play Peek-a-Boo
- ❑ Push Buttons
- ❑ Stack Blocks
- ❑ Clap Hands
- ❑ Pat Objects, Pictures, or Legs
- ❑ Drink from a Sippy Cup
- ❑ Drink from a Straw
- ❑ Walk Backward/Forward in a Walker
- ❑ Rock Back and Forth in Chair/Rocking Toy
- ❑ Scoot Forward/Backward on a Toy Scooter
- ❑ Pick Up Toys
- ❑ Turn Pages in a Book
- ❑ Turn Things On/Off
- ❑ Clap and Dance
- ❑ Point to Objects
- ❑ Match Objects
- ❑ Go Down a Slide
- ❑ Take Objects In/Out of Containers
- ❑ Move Objects from One Container to the Next
- ❑ Nest Objects Inside One Another
- ❑ Give High/Low Fives
- ❑ Walk
- ❑ Run
- ❑ Jump
- ❑ Climb Stairs
- ❑ Drink from a Regular Cup
- ❑ Place a Sippy Cup in a Cup Holder
- ❑ Find an Object under a Blanket
- ❑ Sing Along to Songs
- ❑ Recognize Self in a Picture
- ❑ Recognize Family Members in a Picture
- ❑ Kick a Ball
- ❑ Bounce a Ball
- ❑ Roll a Ball
- ❑ Throw a Ball
- ❑ String Beads on Shoelace
- ❑ Fold Paper
- ❑ Scribble

☐ _____
☐ _____
☐ _____
☐ _____
☐ _____
☐ _____
☐ _____
☐ _____
☐ _____
☐ _____
☐ _____
☐ _____
☐ _____

Action Words

Big	Small	Kiss
Stop	Go	Hug
Fast	Slow	Cuddle
Push	Pull	Hold
Open	Close	Carry
Walk	Run	Hand Me
Stand	Sit	Bring Me
Stand Up	Sit Down	Talk
Look	Listen	Build
See	Blink	Make
Peek	Peek-a-Boo	Stack
Hide	Find	Wait
Smell	Taste	Rest
Touch	Don't Touch	March
Sleep	Awake	Leap
Clean	Dirty	Press
Wash	Wipe	Crush
Cut	Peel	Click
Break	Fix	Cling
Jump	Kick	Stick
Catch	Throw	Bury
Roll	Bounce	Tap
Clap	Dance	Squeeze
Eat	Drink	Squirt
Chew	Swallow	Spit
Blow	Suck	Whistle
Turn	Turn Around	Wear
Roll	Roll Over	Scream

Twist	Spin	Hiss
Climb	Crawl	Howl
Dress	Undress	Growl
Brush	Comb	Knock
Grow	Shrink	Stretch
Give	Take	Hunt
Swim	Float	Explore
Fly	Ride	Hang

Color and Shapes Objectives

Importance:

Colors and shapes are everywhere! They help us identify objects, logos, and signs, and they can even be a way to express our feelings. Color in particular can influence our emotional state and can even impact our ability to think and learn. Shapes allow us to differentiate between objects.

Goals:

To help your child recognize the basic colors and shapes to enhance his or her ability to relate to the world and the objects around him or her

Material Explanation:

Checklist of colors and shapes to work on with your child and mark off as your child masters a particular color or shape

The How-Tos of Colors and Shapes

Start slow. Learning the concepts of color and shape takes time. It takes an even longer amount of time to recognize the different colors and shapes. Start by introducing only a couple of colors or shapes at a time. However, be careful *not* to focus on only one color or one shape at a time, as your child may quickly become bored and disengage from the activity. Instead, try starting with a couple of the primary colors—red, yellow, or blue—and a couple of the basic shapes—a circle, square, or triangle—as these are easily recognizable colors and shapes. Imagine how hard it would be for a young child to easily recognize the difference between a circle and an oval as opposed to a circle and a triangle, or the difference between the colors red and orange as opposed to red and blue. It is a well-known fact that children respond better to primary colors and contrasting colors, for instance, black and white, black and red, or green and white. Once your child has learned the easily recognizable colors and shapes, move on from there.

On Tuesdays, put the entire focus on colors and shapes, whether it's all day or just the forty-five minutes you set aside specifically for preschool. Use these suggestions to get started:

- Point to an object that is red and say, "This is red." Then point to a blue object and say, "This is blue."
- Allow your child to hold the object, and then say something like, "Here, you have the red one, and I'll have the blue one."
- Sort the objects together by their color or shape and talk about the different colors and shapes.
- Utilize toys your child may already have for this objective, such as blocks, rings, stacking cups, etc.
- Utilize common things around the house for this objective, such as dishes, clothes, books, or magazines.
- Go on a scavenger hunt around your house or outside to find a particular color or shape.
- Have a color day when clothes, dishes, art and crafts, etc. are of a particular color; have other members of your family join in.
- Take your child to an art gallery or museum as a field trip.

The idea here is for you, the teacher, to focus on activities and play to enhance learning about colors and shapes. I encourage you to spend forty-five minutes of quality time with your child to help him or her recognize the different colors and shapes. Use the suggested color and shapes checklist to guide you on what colors and shapes to start teaching your child and mark them off as your child masters a particular color or shape. Use the spaces provided to add your own colors and shapes as your child's skills develop. Follow this up by watching a video and/or reading a book related to colors or shapes.

*** Remember, every child is different and everyone learns at different rates. If your child is not mastering a particular color or shape or is becoming frustrated with trying, simply move on to a different color or shape and come back to that one later. The checklist is in no particular order, so you can tailor it to your child as time will allow and as your child's skills develop.

Color and Shapes Trivia Tuesdays

- ❑ Red
- ❑ Blue
- ❑ Yellow
- ❑ Green
- ❑ Purple
- ❑ Orange
- ❑ Brown
- ❑ Black
- ❑ White
- ❑ Pink

- ❑ Circle
- ❑ Square
- ❑ Triangle
- ❑ Rectangle
- ❑ Oval
- ❑ Heart
- ❑ Diamond
- ❑ Star
- ❑ Octagon
- ❑ Pentagon
- ❑ _____
- ❑ _____
- ❑ _____
- ❑ _____
- ❑ _____
- ❑ _____
- ❑ _____
- ❑ _____
- ❑ _____
- ❑ _____
- ❑ _____
- ❑ _____
- ❑ _____
- ❑ _____
- ❑ _____
- ❑ _____

Animal Objectives

Importance:
Animals are an important aspect of human life. They play a significant role in our ecosystem to keep the balance of nature intact. They provide us with food, clothing, and comfort, and they can even have healing benefits. Teaching children about animals and how to love them and take care of them can help ensure the animals in our environment today will be around for generations to come.

Goals:
To help your child recognize many different animals, the parts of the animals, what they eat, and where they live, and to encourage a life-long love for animals

Material Explanation:
Checklist of animals to work on with your child and mark off as your child learns a particular animal, and a blank area for you to add other animals you would like your child to learn about
A generic list of what those animals may eat, to be used as a supplemental learning tool

The How-Tos of Animals

Animals! How fun. This will probably become a favorite subject with your child, as children tend to be intrigued by animals and are very curious about them and their habitats. Introduce a wide variety of animals to your child, including, but not limited to, farm animals, zoo animals, and sea creatures. Engage in real-life (safe) encounters with animals and allow your child to explore and compare the differences between the animals. Talk to your child about what sounds each of the animals make, what each animal eats, and where each animal lives.

On Wednesdays, put the entire focus on animals, whether it's all day or just the forty-five minutes you set aside specifically for preschool. Allow your toddler to interact with both fake and real animals (supervised). Use these suggestions to get started:
Gather and utilize all of your child's stuffed animals to play with and use as a learning tool.

- Play with animal figurines that your child may have, show your child how the animals move, make the sounds the animals make, and pretend the animals are eating what those animals would eat.
- Group the animals together in different orders.
  - o Farm animals, zoo animals, forest animals, etc.
  - o Animals that walk on four legs, animals that walk on two legs.
- Hang animal pictures or posters on the wall.
- Look at animal books or magazines and talk about the animals—what they are doing and their habitats.
- Sing animal songs to your child, including classic nursery rhymes, or make up your own songs!
- Spend quality time with well-behaved pets.
- Pretend to be a particular animal and encourage your child to pretend with you—for instance, hop like a bunny, waddle like a penguin, roar like a tiger.
- Take your child to a circus, a zoo, or a small petting zoo; visit a farm, a pet store, or an animal shelter as a field trip.

The idea here is for you, the teacher, to focus on activities and play to enhance learning about animals. I encourage you to spend forty-five minutes of quality time with your child and focus on activities related to learning about the different kinds of animals, their habits, and their habitats. Use the suggested animal checklist to mark off the animals once your child can clearly identify them, and add your own animals in the extra spaces provided. Also provided as a supplemental learning tool is a generic list of what those animals may eat; it is a simplified list designed with young audiences in mind. Follow this up by watching a video and/or reading a book related to animals.

*** Remember, every child is different and everyone learns at different rates. If your child is having trouble identifying a particular animal, simply move on to a different animal and come back to that one later. The checklists are alphabetized for your convenience but are intended for you to tailor them to your child as time allows and as your child's skills develop.

Animals Gone Wild Wednesdays

Pets

Bird	Gerbil	
Cat	Hamster	
Dog	Mouse	
Ferret	Rabbit	
Fish	Rat	

Farm Animals

Alpaca	Goat	
Chicken	Goose	
Cow	Horse	
Donkey	Pig	
Duck	Sheep	

Zoo Animals

Ape	Kangaroo	
Camel	Leopard	
Cheetah	Lion	
Chimpanzee	Monkey	
Elephant	Panther	
Giraffe	Rhino	
Gorilla	Tiger	
Hippo	Zebra	

Sea Creatures

Crab	Seal	
Dolphin	Sea Turtle	
Jellyfish	Shark	
Lobster	Starfish	
Manatee	Stingray	
Octopus	Walrus	
Seahorse	Whale	

Forest Animals

Bear	Porcupine	
Black Bear	Possum	
Brown Bear	Raccoon	
Chipmunk	Skunk	
Deer	Squirrel	
Fox	Wolf	

Bugs

Ant	Caterpillar	
Bee	Dragonfly	
Bug	Firefly	
Bumblebee	Fly	
Butterfly	Ladybug	

Reptiles and Other Animals

Alligator	Snail	
Frog	Snake	
Lizard	Turtle	
Spider	Worm	

Birds

Blue Jay	Parakeet	
Crow	Parrot	
Dove	Penguin	
Eagle	Pigeon	
Flamingo	Robin	
Macaw	Swan	
Ostrich	Toucan	
Owl	Turkey	

Baby Animals

Bunny	Foal	
Calf	Kid	
Chick	Kitten	
Cub	Lamb	
Duckling	Piglet	
Fawn	Puppy	

What Pets Eat

Animal	Well-Known Food	Other Foods	
Bird (see What Birds Eat)	Worms	Seeds	Berries
Cat	Mouse	Cat Food	Fish
Dog	Dog Bones	Dog Food	Meat
Ferret	Ferret Food		
Fish	Worms	Fish Food	Flies
Gerbil	Seeds	Fruits & Veggies	Grains
Hamster	Seeds	Cereals	Veggies
Mouse	Cheese	Fruits & Veggies	Grains
Rabbit	Carrots	Fruits & Veggies	Grass
Rat	Cheese	Fruits & Veggies	Grains

What Farm Animals Eat

Animal	Well-Known Food	Other Foods		
Alpaca	Grass			Hay
Chicken	Grain	Grass	Seeds	Bugs
Cow	Grass		Grain	Hay
Donkey	Grass		Straw	Flowers
Duck	Fish Bugs	Fruits & Veggies	Aquatic Plants	
Goat	Grass	Alfalfa Hay	Almost Anything!	
Goose	Grass	Leaves	Grain	Aquatic Plants
Horse	Grass	Grain Hay	Apples	Carrots
Pig	Mush (slop)	Corn	Fruits & Veggies	
Sheep	Grass	Clover	Forbs	Grain

What Zoo Animals Eat

Animal	Well-Known Food	Other Foods		
Ape	Bananas	Fruits	Plants	Nuts
Camel	Grass	Dried	Leaves	Seeds
Cheetah	Meat	Antelope	Gazelles	Zebra
Chimpanzee	Fruits	Nuts	Seeds	Insects
Elephant	Plants	Grass Leaves	Bark	Twigs
Giraffe	Leaves			Twigs
Gorilla	Fruit		Vines	Leaves
Hippo	Grass		Water	Plants
Kangaroo	Grass			Leaves
Leopard	Meat	Monkeys	Rodents	Fish
Lion	Meat	Zebra	Buffalo	Antelope
Monkey	Bananas	Fruits	Leaves	Seeds
Panther	Meat		Deer	Raccoons
Rhino	Grass		Leaves	Twigs
Tiger	Meat	Antelope	Deer	Boars
Zebra	Grass	Leaves	Twigs	Bark

What Sea Creatures Eat

Sea Creature	Well-Known Food			Other Foods	
Crab	Algae				Fungi
Dolphin	Fish				Squid
Jellyfish	Fish				Plankton
Lobster	Crabs				Fish
Manatee	Seaweed				
Octopus	Crabs	Clams	Snails	Fish	Shrimp
Seahorse	Fish (small)			Shrimp (small)	
Seal	Fish				Squid
Sea Turtle	Sea Grass			Jellyfish	Shrimp
Shark	Fish			Seals	Plankton
Starfish	Clams			Oysters	Fish
Stingray	Clams				Fish
Walrus	Clams			Crabs	Snail
Whale	Fish	Seals	Sea Lions	Marine Animals	

What Forest Animals Eat

Animal	Well-Known Food	Other Foods
Bear	Fish	Berries
Black Bear	Honey	Nuts Berries Fish
Brown Bear	Fish	Berries
Chipmunk	Nuts Seeds	
Deer	Plants Leaves Grass Twigs	Nuts
Fox	Rabbits Mice	Insects Fruit
Porcupine	Plants Bark Twigs	Leaves
Possum	Fruit	Insects
Raccoon	Berries	Nuts Seeds
Skunk	Insects	Fruit Rats
Squirrel	Nuts	Seeds Fruit
Wolf	Deer Rabbits Mice Birds	Fish

What Bugs Eat

Bug	Well-Known Food	Other Foods
Ant	Almost Anything	Sugar
Bee	Pollen	Nectar
Bumblebee	Nectar	Pollen
Butterfly	They drink liquids rather than eat	
Caterpillar	Plants	
Dragonfly	Flies	Mosquitoes
Firefly	Snails	Slugs
Fly	Nectar	
Ladybug	Aphids (a small green insect)	

What Reptiles and Other Animals Eat

Reptile	Well-Known Food			Other Foods
Alligator	Meat	Fish	Birds	Turtles
Frog	Insects			Worms
Lizard	Insects			
Spider	Insects			
Snail	Plants		Leaves	Flowers
Snake	Mice		Insects	Eggs
Turtle (general)	Plants			Meat
Worm	Dirt			Plants

What Birds Eat

Bird	Well Known Food		Other Foods
Blue Jay	Seeds		Nuts
Crow	Corn	Fruit	Nuts
Dove	Seeds		Worms
Eagle	Fish	Ducks	Snakes
Flamingo	Shrimp		Insects
Macaw	Nuts	Seeds	Fruit
Ostrich	Seeds	Leaves	Flowers
Owl	Mice	Rabbits	Squirrels
Parakeet	Seeds		Veggies
Parrot	Seeds	Fruits	Veggies
Penguin	Fish		Squid
Robin	Worms		Fruit
Swan	Aquatic Plants		Grass

Toucan	Tropical Fruits	Nuts
Turkey	Seeds Nuts	Berries

What Baby Animals Drink

Animal	Well-Known Food		Other Foods
Bunny	Milk		
Calf	Milk		
Chick	Chick Starter		Insects
Cub	Milk		
Duckling	Duck Starter	Insects	Worms
Fawn	Milk		
Foal	Milk		
Kid	Milk		
Kitten	Milk		
Lamb	Milk		
Piglet	Milk		
Puppy	Milk		

Number Objectives

Importance:
Numbers are the building blocks for mathematics and will play an important role in your child's life. Numbers are a part of our everyday lives. Without numbers, we would not be able to read a clock, know how fast we are driving, or purchase items at the store. We would not be able to call someone on the telephone or even pay our bills. By teaching your child about numbers, you are not only preparing your child for the world, but you could also be building the foundation for a future job or career.

Goals:
To help your child recognize numbers, count out loud, and begin to physically count objects in order to place a value on the amount of something

Material Explanation:
A checklist of numbers to work on with your child and mark off as your child learns to recognize a particular number
A list of goals to achieve

The How-Tos of Numbers

Count, count, count! Count out loud, sing counting songs, count objects, look for numbers, read numbers . . . the more experiences your child has with hearing, seeing, and using numbers, the easier it will be for your child to understand that there is a value to the amount of something.

On Thursdays, put the entire focus on numbers, whether it's all day or just the forty-five minutes you set aside specifically for preschool. Incorporate numbers into your child's activities and use these suggestions to get started:

- Count out loud to your child, repeatedly.
- Allow your child to observe you counting objects.
- Point to numbers and say them in order, backward, or individually.
- Hold up your fingers while counting and/or use one hand to count the fingers on your other hand.
- Draw big numbers on paper or a dry-erase board and ask your child what number it is, or to point out a number from a series of numbers.
- Use sidewalk chalk outside to draw numbers and then ask your child to touch, step on, or jump on a particular number.
- Ask your child how many he or she has of something and then count how many your child has (e.g., crayons he or she is holding).
- Try to find numbers in every room of your house with your child.
  - o   Look at clocks, scales, timers, TV remotes, phones, etc.
- March to numbers, counting out loud for your child as you march.
  - o   Include musical instruments or twirl objects.
- Match numbers with your child. Have two identical sets of numbers and ask your child to find the matching number.
- Take your child and his or her piggy bank to the bank as a field trip.

The idea here is for you, the teacher, to focus activities and play to enhance learning about numbers and how to count. I encourage you to spend forty-five minutes of quality time with your child and focus on saying, recognizing, and counting numbers. Use the suggested number checklist to mark off the numbers once your child can clearly identify that number, and use the three focus objectives as a guide. Follow this up by watching a video and/or reading a book related to numbers.

*** Remember, every child is different and everyone learns at different rates. If your child is not mastering a particular number or is becoming frustrated with trying to learn a particular number, simply move on to a different number and come back to that one later.

Thinking Numbers Thursdays

  1
  2
  3
  4
  5
  6
  7
  8
  9
  10

Recognize the numbers 1–10
Count out loud to 10
Begin to physically count objects

** If your child masters all of these goals, begin to introduce the numbers 11–20.

Fun Friday Objectives

Importance:
Simply having fun with your child is an important bonding mechanism. Bonding and building a good, strong relationship with your children may help your children feel more secure about themselves and may allow them to have the confidence they need to come to you in the future when they need help.

Goals:
To get out of the house and have fun or simply take a break from learning and just enjoy time with your child

Whether you go out or stay in, simply enjoy your child without focusing on learning or any preschool activities

Material Explanation:
Suggested ideas to do with your child to have fun and take a break from preschool

The How-Tos of Having Fun

Take a break! You have worked hard all week and so has your child. This day is intended for you and your child to simply have fun and enjoy one another. Get out of the house, make a craft, or simply play at home. Whatever you decide, ensure you reserve some quality time for you and your child to have fun together!

On Fridays, put the entire focus on having fun, whether it's all day or just the forty-five minutes you would normally set aside specifically for preschool. Allow your toddler to be included in the decision-making process or perhaps surprise him or her with an activity you have planned. Here are some suggested guidelines to follow:

- Safety always comes first! Be sure to choose an activity that is safe for your child to participate in.
- If you or your child is not feeling well, reserve fun activities for a time when you are both feeling better.
- Try to choose a different activity every week.
- Try to get out of the house with your child if possible.
  - o Toddlers love experiencing the world and seeing new things.
  - o This time out of the house will benefit both you and your child.
  - o Remember, there are lots of activities outside the home that cost little or no money. Try experiencing activities in nature.
- **Field Trip Ideas:** See the "Go Out" section.

The idea here is for you, the teacher, to focus on fun activities. I encourage you to spend forty-five minutes of quality time with your child and simply have fun, with no preschool curriculum to follow. Use the suggested having fun checklist to give you ideas to relax, have fun, and enjoy time with your child. Add your own ideas in the spaces provided. Follow this up by watching a video and/or reading a book related to the activity you and your child did on this day; however, if that is not possible due to resources, simply talk to your child about the fun activity you shared together.

*** Remember, every child is different and everyone has different moods at different times. If your child or you are not experiencing a fun time with the activity that was decided on, simply move on to a different activity and come back to that one at a later time. The checklist is in no particular order. It is intended to provide only suggestions so you and your child can have the flexibility to choose whatever activity you like.

Fun Fridays

Go Out
- ❑ Go to the Park
- ❑ Go to the Library
- ❑ Go to a Bookstore
- ❑ Go to the Mall
- ❑ Go Shopping
- ❑ Go out to Eat
- ❑ Go to the Pet Store
- ❑ Go on a Picnic
- ❑ Take a Walk
- ❑ Visit Family or Friends
- ❑ Enjoy Mother Nature

Stay In
- ❑ Make a Craft
  - o See the "Arts & Crafts" section.
- ❑ Play Games
  - o See the "Games to Play" section.
- ❑ Pretend Play
  - o Introduce pretend play to your child. Pretend to be animals, your child's favorite character, or a doctor or fireman.
- ❑ Play Dress-Up
- ❑ Play, Play, Play Whatever *Your* Child Chooses!

- ❑ _____
- ❑ _____
- ❑ _____

ABCs Objectives

Importance:
Language is the key to human communication. It is our tool for transferring information and expressing our thoughts, ideas, feelings, and emotions. In the English language, the alphabet is the fundamental building block of literacy. Learning to read and write involves letter recognition and the ability to translate letters into speech sounds.

Goals:
To help your child recognize objects and words to better communicate with the world, and to introduce the alphabet to your child

Material Explanation:
A checklist of the letters in the alphabet to mark off as your child recognizes each letter
A checklist of words to work on with your child and mark off as your child understands each word and its meaning and/or its related object
A blank area for you to add words you would like to work on with your child

The How-Tos of ABCs

Take some time! This is an area that takes time, practice, and patience. Even if your child is only saying a few words right now, more than likely, your child can understand a lot more words than he or she can say, and this can be very frustrating to a young child who is trying to communicate his or her needs and wants. As a parent, you can do certain things to help your child become less frustrated, learn to communicate in a positive manner (instead of crying or throwing temper tantrums), and begin to understand more of the world around him or her. There is a lot your child will need to learn in order to efficiently communicate with others and know the world around him or her, so it is very important for you to approach this material with patience and understanding.

On Saturdays, put the entire focus on language, whether it's all day or just the forty-five minutes you set aside specifically for preschool. Open the lines of communication up to your toddler by sharing with him or her your knowledge about speech and his or her environment. Use these suggestions to get started:

- Point out objects to your child and name the objects. Allow your child to touch or hold each object if possible.
    - o   Do this throughout the various rooms in your house and outside.
- View picture books with your child and discuss what you and your child see.
- Quiz your child by asking your child to touch, point, or bring you a particular object.
- Repeatedly sing the alphabet song to your child or allow your child to listen to it from a recording.
- Place an alphabet chart at your child's eye level.
    - o   Point to the letters as you name them for your child.
    - o   Ask your child to find particular letters.
- Write letters on a chalkboard, dry-erase board, or paper for your child; name the letters or quiz your child on the letters.
- Read to your child on a daily basis.
    - o   This does not teach your child how to read; however, it allows your child to hear words that are not normally spoken in everyday language.
    - o   This will help your child learn that there is a correlation between the written word and the spoken language.
    - o   If you can run your finger under the words as you read books, this can help your child understand that we read from left to right.
    - o   This can also show your child how to turn the pages of a book.
- Rhyme to your child: at, bat, cat, sat, mat, pat . . .
- Build your child's tongue, mouth, and jaw muscles by moving your tongue and/or mouth various ways and encouraging your child to mimic your actions.
- Take your child to a library or a bookstore as a field trip.

The idea here is for you, the teacher, to focus on activities and play to enhance learning letters and words. I encourage you to spend forty-five minutes of quality time with your child and focus on activities related to language and communication. Use the alphabet chart to mark off the letters as your child learns each letter, and use the suggested word list to guide you on what words to start teaching to your child. Mark the words off as your child understands the meaning of each particular one. Follow this up by watching a video and/or reading a book related to language.

*** Remember, every child is different and everyone learns at different rates. If your child is not mastering a particular word or letter, simply move on to a different word or letter and come back to that one later. The checklist is in no particular order, so you can tailor it to your child, as time will allow and as your child's skills develop.

ABCs Saturdays

- [ ] A
- [ ] B
- [ ] C
- [ ] D
- [ ] E
- [ ] F
- [ ] G
- [ ] H
- [ ] I
- [ ] J
- [ ] K
- [ ] L
- [ ] M
- [ ] N
- [ ] O
- [ ] P
- [ ] Q
- [ ] R
- [ ] S
- [ ] T
- [ ] U
- [ ] V
- [ ] W
- [ ] X
- [ ] Y
- [ ] Z

People

Aunt	Grandma	
Baby	Grandpa	
Brother	Mommy	
Cousin	Sister	
Daddy	Uncle	

Objects

Airplane	Comb	
Animal	House	
Ball	Keys	
Boat	Phone	
Book	Table	
Brush	Train	
Car	Truck	
Chair	Toy	

Clothes

Coat	Pants	
Dress	Shirt	
Hat	Shoes	
Mittens	Socks	
Pajamas	Swimsuit	

Mealtime

Bib	Eat	
Bottle	Fork	
Bowl	Highchair	
Cereal	Juice	
Chair	Milk	
Cracker	Napkin	
Cup	Plate	
Drink	Snack	

Bedtime

Awake	Moon	
Bed	Nighttime	
Bedtime Story	Pillow	
Blanket	Sleep	
Crib	Stars	

Body Parts

Arms	Head	
Ears	Legs	
Eyes	Mouth	
Feet	Nose	
Hair	Teeth	
Hands	Toes	

Actions

Bring Me	Lay Down	
Come Here	Open/Close	
Dance	Peek-a-Boo	
Give Me	Sit Down	
Hi/Bye	Stand Up	
Hug	Turn On/Off	
I Love You!	Wave	
Kiss	Where Is?	
Kiss Me	Yes/No	

Other Words

Sunday School's Objectives

Importance:
To provide your child with hope and strengthen him or her as an individual, a family member and a productive member of society.

Goals:
To familiarize your child with the religion, beliefs, and customs of your family

Material Explanation:
There is no checklist with this material, as there are so many different types of religion. Use the "How-Tos" section of this chapter to give you ideas to introduce religion into your child's life

The How-Tos of Sunday School

Optional material! If you choose to introduce a higher power or spiritual being into your child's life, reserve this day to partake in activities to teach your child some basic ideas and concepts related to your religion of choice.

Focus on basic practices, beliefs, words, and significant beings related to your religion, and allow your child to worship with you and partake in general practices. Set good examples for your child by following the practices and beliefs you wish your child to follow and learn. Think about the most important aspects of your religion and introduce those to your child first. More specific details can be introduced at a later time as your child grows. Use these suggestions to get started:

- Take your child to worship with you.
- Spend time alone with your child to worship and talk about your religion.
- Pray with your child—at mealtime, before bed, etc.
- Show your child pictures relevant to your religion.
- Read age-appropriate books relevant to your religion.
- Visit a church or different churches, or take your child to Sunday school or Vacation Bible School.

The idea here is for you, the teacher, to focus on activities and play to enhance learning the religion of your choice. I encourage you to spend forty-five minutes of quality time with your child and focus on activities related to your religion and help your child understand its basic beliefs and practices. Follow this up by watching a video and/or reading a book related to your religion of choice.

*** Remember, every child is different and everyone learns at different rates. If your child is not mastering a particular aspect of your religion, simply move on to a different one and come back to that one later. Depending on your faith and religion, you may choose to work on this subject throughout the entire week.

Music Time Objectives

Importance:
Music can influence our emotional state in a way that can alter both our emotions and our behavior. Music can calm, sooth, anger, motivate, lift our spirits, bring back memories, or help us express how we feel. Introducing music to your child at a very young age can have long-lasting effects on your child's life. Exposing your child to the appropriate kinds of music at an early age can also help mold who he or she becomes and teach him or her many things.

Goals:
To expose your child to a wide variety of music and to introduce an array of musical instruments, song, and dance that will encourage emotional growth

Material Explanation:
Suggested variety of music to expose your child to, including a blank area for you to add your own musical choices

The How-Tos of Music Time

Music Time! Get movin' and groovin' with your toddler while enjoying the wonderful world of music. You will quickly discover that your toddler will love listening to music, such as classic nursery rhymes and other children's songs, and your toddler will love making music himself or herself. (Even though it may sound like noise to us!)

Whenever you feel like it, set aside time to focus on music. While just listening to the radio may be beneficial for exposing your toddler to different types of music, such as country, soft rock, etc., a greater benefit can come from experiencing music hands on. Although toddlers do learn by watching and listening to others, my belief is that children gain more value from actually experiencing things themselves. Incorporate movement into music time as much as possible to enhance the learning experience. Use these suggestions to get started:

- Clap your hands to music and encourage your child to join in.
- March to music or songs that you sing to your child.
    - Play a musical instrument while you are marching and encourage your child to do the same.
- Act out the motions to classic nursery rhymes and other children's songs. For instance:
    - "The Itsy Bitsy Spider"
    - "I'm a Little Teapot"
    - "Head, Shoulders, Knees, and Toes"
- Allow your child to play with age-appropriate musical instruments, such as a xylophone, drums, maracas, a small piano, or bells. Several of these instruments can be made from things in your home. For instance:
    - Provide your toddler with a wooden spoon and different-sized pots and pans for drums.
    - Fill jars with dry beans or rice and seal the lids tightly for different-sounding shakers.
    - Use aluminum pie pans as cymbals.
- Play musical instruments for your child and allow him or her to join in.
- Introduce your child to the classic game of musical chairs.
- Acquire a wide variety of music to share with your child.
    - The library is an excellent source of music options.
- Take your child to an outdoor concert or children's musical.

The idea here is for you, the teacher, to focus on activities and play to expose your child to different types of music and musical experiences. I encourage you to spend quality time with your child and focus on activities related to experiencing music hands on. Follow this up by talking to your child about the musical experience he or she had, or watching a video and/or reading a book related to music.

*** Remember, every child is different and everyone learns at different rates. If your child is not interested in a particular musical instrument or music activity, simply explore a different musical instrument or activity. The checklist is in no particular order so you can tailor it to your child, as time will allow and as your child's skills develop.

Music Time Anytime

Expose your child to a wide variety of music.

- ❑ Classical Music
- ❑ Nursery Rhymes
- ❑ Lullabies
- ❑ Toddler Music and Other Children's Songs
- ❑ Soft Rock
- ❑ Dance Music
- ❑ Radio
- ❑ Live Music
    - o Family, Friends, or Yourself (depending on your own talents)
- ❑ Holiday Music
- ❑ Sing to Your Child
    - o Even if your singing voice isn't the greatest, your child will enjoy listening to you.
- ❑ Make Up Your Own Songs to Sing to Your Child
- ❑ Make Up Your Own Dances to Teach Your Child

- ❑ _____
- ❑ _____
- ❑ _____
- ❑ _____
- ❑ _____

Arts and Crafts

- ❖ Painting
  - o Yes, it's messy! But the rewards are well worth the mess. Children who actively paint can get a sense of accomplishment and self-worth. To them, each painting is a work of art. Painting is a learning process that teaches children about colors and how they can be mixed, along with teaching cause and effect and motor skills.
  - o To the very young artist, painting is more about feeling, not so much about what the final product looks like. Never discourage a child from painting how he or she wants and try not to guide his or her direction, as this is the child's artwork, not yours.
  - o For children still using a highchair, tape a piece of construction paper to their highchair tray after mealtime and provide a couple drops of different colored water-based finger paints. Talk to your child about the colors and how it feels on his or her fingers. A bib or painting smock and some baby wipes make cleanup easier.
    - ❖ For children who only seem interested in eating the paint, try allowing them to paint with vanilla or chocolate pudding and then try water-based paints later.
  - o As your child gets older, tape or hold a piece of paper for him or her at a table and provide brushes, sponges, or other safe objects he or she can dip into the paint. Pie pans, paper plates, or small plastic containers work well for this. A bowl of warm, soapy water for painting utensils and some baby wipes make cleanup easier.
  - o As your child grows, you may choose to introduce an easel or body painting. Both can be done outside on a sidewalk with water-based paints for easier cleanup.
    - ❖ Body painting can be accomplished by rolling paint onto children's hands or feet and allowing them to walk across a big piece of paper or by helping them "stamp" their handprint onto a piece of paper or other material.
      - • Be sure to hold onto your children's hands and help support them after painting their feet so they do not slip or fall, as paint is very slippery.

- ❖ Stamping
  - o Tape a piece of paper to a table and provide your child with water-based ink and stamps. At first, this will consist of random stamping, but eventually you can show your child how to make activity scenes using the different stamps you may have.
    - ❖ A little practice and help from you will be necessary to teach your child that he or she first needs to "stamp" the stamp onto the inkpad and then onto paper. Practice makes perfect!

❖ Coloring
  o Allow your child to use a wide variety of oversized crayons to color on different types of paper.
  o Talk to your child about the colors and what colors show up on the different types of paper (for instance, white crayons show up on black paper).
  o Experiment with using different colors on top of each other to make other colors (e.g., red and yellow make orange).
  o Provide coloring pages with large shapes or drawings and encourage your child to color them in or simply to stay inside the lines.

❖ Sidewalk Chalk
  o Take it outside! Offer your child different colors and types of sidewalk chalk.
  o Talk about the colors.
  o Show your child how you can draw objects with the chalk.
  o Encourage your child to make marks and color in the objects that you have drawn for him or her.
  o Experiment with using chalk on paper, especially black paper.
  o Take preschool outside with chalk!
     ❖ For animals day, draw animals with chalk and talk about the animals and the sounds they make.
     ❖ For numbers day, draw numbers or hopscotch, or simply count the drawings.
        • Encourage your child to step on the said number or hop on the said hopscotch number.
        • Example: "Can you step on the number four?"

❖ Play Dough
  o Kids love play dough! What a fun way to interact with your child and work on motor skills.
  o Sit at a table with your child and provide safe tools (store-bought or homemade) to practice stamping, cutting, and creating objects with play dough.
  o Talk about the colors, the shapes, and how the play dough feels in between your fingers. Also smell it . . . but don't taste it!
     ❖ Never leave a young child alone with play dough.
     ❖ Use care around carpet because play dough may stain.
  o This is a recipe for play dough:
        • 1 cup flour
        • 1 cup warm water
        • ¼ cup salt
        • 2 tsp. cream of tartar
        • 1 tsp. oil food coloring
     Mix first five ingredients, add food coloring, and then stir on medium heat until blended. Remove from heat and knead until well blended. Place leftovers in airtight bags or containers.

❖ Gluing
  o This is one of the more difficult activities for children at this age to understand and do. Attempt this activity when your child is closer to two years of age.
  o Allow your child to practice using a washable glue stick to glue precut paper objects to a piece of construction paper to make a collage.
      ❖ If possible, use a glue stick that applies in color but dries clear.
      ❖ Show your child how to turn the paper objects over, apply the glue, sit the glue stick down, use both hands to flip the object over and place on the construction paper, and then pat it down.

Games to Play

- ❖ Peek-a-Boo
- ❖ Hide and Seek
- ❖ Follow the Leader
- ❖ Simon Says
- ❖ Get You or Catch You
    - o This is where you *safely* chase your child and pretend to "get" him or her. (They love that!)
- ❖ Matching Games
- ❖ Puzzles: wooden or big, simple cardboard puzzles
- ❖ Hidden Object/Scavenger Hunt
    - o This is where you hide simple objects and ask your child to find them, sort of like an Easter egg hunt.

Don't forget, lots and lots of tickles and laughter!

Materials to purchase or make that may be beneficial to this curriculum

Wooden Puzzles
    Motor Skills
    Colors and Shapes
    Numbers
    Letters

Books
    Colors and Shapes
    Animals
    Numbers
    Letters

Videos
    Colors and Shapes
    Animals
    Numbers
    Letters

Flash Cards
    Colors and Shapes
    Animals
    Numbers
    Letters

Animal Figurines
    Animals
    Numbers

Alphabet Chart
    Letters

Number Chart
    Numbers

Coloring Books and Large Crayons
    Colors and Shapes
    Motor Skills

Water-Based Finger Paints, Paint Brushes, and Sponges
    Colors and Shapes
    Motor Skills

Water-Based Markers
> Colors and Shapes
> Motor Skills

Water-Based Ink Pads and Stamps
> Colors and Shapes
> Motor Skills

Play Dough
> Colors and Shapes
> Motor Skills

Stickers
> Motor Skills

*** Remember, every child is different and everyone learns at different rates. If your child is not interested in participating in a particular game or art and craft activity, simply explore a different activity and come back to that one at a later time.

I encourage you to play with your child, learn with them, have fun together and focus!

Printed in the United States
By Bookmasters